Indigena Awry

Indigena

Awry

Annharte

VANCOUVER | NEW STAR BOOKS | 2015

NEW STAR BOOKS LTD.
107 — 3477 Commercial Street
Vancouver, BC V5N 4E8   CANADA

1574 Gulf Road, No. 1517
Point Roberts, WA 98281   USA

www.NewStarBooks.com
info@NewStarBooks.com

The publisher acknowledges the financial support of the Canada Council for the Arts, the Government of Canada through the Canada Book Fund, the British Columbia Arts Council, and the Government of British Columbia through the Book Publishing Tax Credit.

Cataloguing information for this book is available from Library and Archives Canada, www.collectionscanada.gc.ca.

Cover design: Mark Mushet
Cover image: Lawrence Paul Yuxweluptun, "Lost My Legend Downtown Last Night", National Gallery of Canada, Ottawa.
Printed on recycled paper
Printed and bound in Canada by Imprimerie Gauvin, Gatineau, QC
First printing, November 2012. Reprinted 2015.

Contents

as if one bear

commie conversations

tweak

In honour

Forrest Funmaker Hap honi	Dayseeker (Lifeseeker)
Madeline Terbasket Manape Mani Wi	Walking Soldier Woman
Soffia Funmaker Huc xununik	Little Bear
Jalen Funmaker Coni mani	First Walker

mixed bag

soft spoken bitch

Silence is a girl who once was in Winnipeg. She was a kid who lived on the same block half breeds occupied territory. In sunshine, rhinestones paved the back lane. She played without cutting her feet on the broken wine and beer bottles. Footwear was canvas tennis shoes with sparkles on the soles. Not beaded moccasins but close enough.

Silence never did enjoy the sound of a wince or whine. She got very tall but kept being a timid little girl. Her mouth kept shut. She displayed teenager blackheads on pale face Indian looks. Lucky she got pissed off often. Her complexion turned red in blotches. Hey, part red skin.

No hopes to move up in the world. Not that she could fall in or out of a crack in the system. She was too modest to even notice her own crack. Anyway, she turned out multi cultured and multi coloured without trying that hard.

Apartheid was common in South Africa except one summer she got a good job integrating City Hall. She posed as a Native woman at the front counter. Phones rang all day. Her words kept to a basic minimum. Hello. What Do You Want? Goodbye. With finesse she exacted the perfect justice. Wait for an answer from a muted or mutant Indian? Stand in line. In time, Indian time, she let calls go through. Her other line was too busy so incoming calls kept on hold gave her intense pleasure. She shared her heritage of waiting for silence to be heard.

Silence even with big girl looks wanted a momma heart. Big hearted and big footed. She would step on a heart then lift it up to comfort obvious pain. Silence took her sweet time to heal injuries inflicted in the game of love. She had a scream that never made it past her big front teeth. Slurred words were not silence even if hard to understand. Drunk words did not fall down on the city sidewalk. Choked words and cramped intestine made her gutsy yet way more than soft spoken bitch.

Her insides were too quiet so she wore loud clothes to work every day of the week. The transparent gown indicated she was on a honeymoon. Just so happy to be working and getting a pay cheque she deserved to earn more often. A velvet dress was for rubbing up others the wrong way. The boss liked her harassment. A blue taffeta shift rustled a Monday morning greeting after a rugged weekend. The right clothes can make a woman outstanding and distinguished. Plain street dress was extreme iffy garb.

Silence had a rowdy next door neighbour. His noise was a bother. Going to sleep was rough. She should of passed out again. Then the sound of a sad tuba drifted through the window one hangover a Saturday morning ago. Not a familiar tune she knew. Yeah, right! Just a pinched off fart coming out of a pinhole asshole.

Toulouse Art Trick

Let us duel. You and me right here not outside. Voyez-vous ça exercise bra? Tits jammed. Still a weapon. Belly gapes from dressing gown, Toulouse. Sash is draped over the chair back. Might tie you up if you want. Aieee, safety pin closure. Fat sticks out. All my fat is me and may intimidate you. If left out of life, fat is company. Forgive me this excess, mon chéri.

Enough me. Back to you, Toulouse. Would you sketch crotched out panty hose? Not a trick question. Oeuvre is Louvre. Here, par exemple, is a pair of black net stockings. Might have kicked can can. Not too careful in pulling on the legs though, me. Hey, the suspense that queen size is not too small. But, did you, Toulouse, only paint mistresses? Stockings of the dancers at the Moulin Rouge were full of runs, n'est-ce pas? Would you devote your best brush strokes to snagged fish nets abandoned by fat ladies? Ever? Would you draw a likeness of me dolling up? My concealed weapon will be my fat.

what do we mean "we"

LR gov't hired gun informed Tonto gov't ploy Tonto had no
recourse but to install silver bullet into chaps playful chap was
he certain skin buckskin curtain beaten heart half broken Tonto
smart enough spied representation twilight lemon lime light
enlighten up

other day Tonto and LR duked it out hey what's with the loin
cloth behind mask infamously acceptable opinion Tonto and LR
exchange fists cuffed connections promoted both violence with
vigilance why anger not laugh tears craze confusion unwashed
masses fear habits

nun and Tonto in movie must watch popcorn closely meanwhile
LR satiated ingrate orders pizza throws up anticipation nothing
distracts like stoic smile Tonto spits unpopped kernels LR greedy
unmasked what they don't know hurts afraid to duck in dark
theatres show must

go ka ching bullet drops slow to reach climax grapple self fumble
other fingers dislodge find turn twist blood stops a sec looks
into camera to say hi to cousins damn one bullet strays this
way across aisles roads ditch superhighways penetrates laser red
safety in shadows we want we mean "we" do want "we" innate
incognita

fly lady fashion

she is me fashion
dame of destiny
she does sneak out

reveal innermost
gets spunky spirited
she wants me spiffy
a dressing me mama

appropriate fashion
unconventional design
she makes me wonder
who is in charge
the catwalk I strut
I will walk like a horse
much more in step with
those lifting shaggy hooves
no spike heels one foot
in front of other glide

she compels me to make a vest
adorned with hearts spilling out top
her choice of hearts works
anything works in quantities
I am to construct accessories
detail patchwork embroider
outline appliqué hearts
show kindness stitch
accent tuft vulnerability
scrap quilt strange romance
attachment bonding built

underneath garment weave
tiny hearts on black white textile

morphing a possibility crosswise
lady trickster cut body one tail
wrongside finesse fantasy encase

her fashion statement will fly
even fly by night match batting
pass for appropriate costume
no bits she will not stop designs
her template takes over
covers moves on my life
upscales yet flatters full
figured modest appearance
day to day she may reside
dormant her schemes kept
a trifle secret even in peril

where is my commander
why am I not suited up
camo fatigues as I walk
the back lane of my block
I expect a mugging robbery
rape beating confrontation
why could I not have donned
mosquito netting protective gear
to meet not so friendly neighbours

she might have encouraged me
to assume the medsin woman look
wear a long skirt with pants
long braid with hidden razor
at the end to help whip slash
any Warrior Hells Angel visage

I must dress brave hearted woman
carry gutting knife at the waist
weaponize high top moccasins
to help me walk in beauty
in a slum when spirit slumps

me over end of trail war pony
exhausted as I am for desperate
grip of Plains Indian stereotype

suddenly she gets insistent
belligerent that I add headwear
a pair of white pantyhose legs
dangling imitation of Hopi clown
she has gone way beyond harlequin
so anticipatory of the next upcoming
Tricksters Ball she forgets I have
a fashion of my own — survival

Squaw Guide

You Audience
Me Squaw
need to practise those lines
it is not the same as Tarzan Jane address
in the old movies
he yelled as he swung out holding his vine
dropped down to deliver commands
to Simba after bossing Cheeta all day

it's not exactly the same either
being called squaw
after going to a high school football game
coming home on the bus
this drunk white hosehead
yells out from the back
there's a squaw sitting up front
no not me — didn't look around — not me
because I grew semi-invisible
nobody noticed I was the only
invisible Indian
going to high school in the city
back in the 50s
unless there were lots even I didn't see

I needed the low self-esteem concept
to explain why nobody was on my side
why nobody told him I belonged
they were being good Canadians
nice he was racist & nice I was the squaw
it didn't make me act up like Jay Silverheels
as if I would speak up to joke
WHAT DO YOU MEAN
WE WHITEBODY

I wasn't Tonto or tough enough
to defer say kemosabe
you had to be tough
a popular Indian Jack Jacobs
Blue Bomber football champion

Aw fuckem if they can't take a joke
a stand up comic would hit hard
in a comeback routine tell off heckler
hey bud you lost a right to get laid
in the westend or northend by a squaw

why not if Tarzan
makes Simba lie down when told
& Cheeta screams pointing to his butt

Ok okay now no more drudge grudge
I'm taking women studies
& that's tough
because I don't have a closet
that's empty enough for me to get inside
think about it I got too many skeletons
the closet is full
haven't counted inventory yet

them bones dem bones
dem shy bones
like the typical squaw in the old days
I was the shy kind
my best friend used to laugh
holding fingers fanned out
hiding her whole self
the big mouth
because it was hard to be a big squaw
big public squaw
I was too invisible to laugh out loud

in the university I go every day
during classes I transform
from text book squaw
who doesn't speak up
I usually do this
scary business when not supposed
to say anything contentious
silence is reward or reworded
everyone looks my way
to check if I am being quiet each day
I might abuse my feminism
switch bitch from academic squaw
to academic sasquatch

as I speak squaws are past tense
used to be but nobody says that word much

hey but wait a minute
did you gaze at me funny
intend just a bit
to call me a squaw?

being a squaw is very demanding
in the movies or on a native production set
it is when a woman gets told
                              make tea squaw
                              braid my hair after
said by a warrior no less

on the rez the women say my chief what my chief says
his speech never mentions my squaws my papooses
now why is that?

it's hard to be a political correct squaw
my secret: don't ever open mouth
or let yawn indicate how boring
better not to say anymore about that

but say the drunken squaw is aggressive best
saw some young women doing some reverse
squaw baiting
they were sitting in a bus shelter
whenever a guy would go by
one of them would say
HEY HUN-NAY
intimidating voice all husky
BOO JOO HUN-NAY
at next pow wow in South Dakota
I would say in breathy tone
WASHTE HUN-NAY

should feminism makes me too shy
to joke around much
them women now talk about outing
wonder out where?
in the bush?

probably out of my mind
like I said
dis closet is all junk
I'm serious
know all inside
intimate me squaw

help me I'm a poor Indian who doesn't have enough books

I am building a barricade. You can help me.
Indigenous people all across the country blocked roads
railways dams
                        held vigils for Kanesatake/Kahnawake
camped in parks, government buildings & on bridges

the Indian Act shoved down our throats   no more silence

each day cousins in crowded cell blocks listened for news
            FREEDOM FOR FIRST NATIONS
mothers & fathers of mothers who fathered fathers mothered
those relatives who didn't build a barricade in their heads

                        disbelief in white people is healthy
believe me

I am seriously building a barricade   first I watched others
parking their "Indian cars" on highways   witnessed the RCMP
pretend help pull them down from cars by pulling feet first
pushed faces to pavement or bashed bodies on car doors with
handfuls of hair they got better grip

                                they let the Indian rookies practise
putting the screws to another Indian person, client, inmate
isn't as racist it proves loyalty

                    but we're not done with each other yet
                    we still have a job to do me and you

help me build another barricade I promise to challenge you

send me your used Kinsellas (even the ones you read & liked)

DANCE ME OUTSIDE

THE MISS HOBBEMA PAGEANT

SCARS

have any Anne Camerons to spare?

DAUGHTERS OF COPPER WOMAN

or one by her alias, Cam Hubert?

DREAMSPEAKER

maybe she'll throw in a few copies
                                    herself
hey scrap the I Wuzza Wannabee
confessional anthology idea
before it comes to mind & print

perchance Lynn Andrews may not help out

let's liberate Agnes Whistling Elk
send used

        MEDICINE WOMAN CRYSTAL WOMAN
        FLIGHT OF THE SEVENTH MOON STAR
          WOMAN
        JAGUAR WOMAN WINDHORSE WOMAN

        is there an Out Of Wind Woman in the house?

        sometimes stolen is as good as used
        try to send the most recent copy
        send me BONE BIRD or Rudy Wiebe's
        THE TEMPTATIONS OF BIG BEAR

the greatest prize is surprise me
this list is too short   be creative
use your imagination   the way they don't

research libraries (tell 'em sorry
gotta take this book for a friend)
like writers in pen international
need liberation so do books from
mental shelves dust collections

you gotta help me build a barricade
wonder how high it will be finished
when me and you stand
from the top
we'll better detect
check out what books a neighbour reads

buffalo jump off the page
predicable end of trail saga
how to save an indigenous group
from consumer envy
write their history right

don't fall for that one no not no more
after we compare notes that's
how we know how it starts
know the best books for barricade

        give me WRITING THE CIRCLE
        dizzy from quick read
            white messiahs made a snare
            grovelling is fun   expressed the right
            way

appropriation
with permission
undermine Indigenous writings
     rip off talents
     rip us apart
     rip into us to see what we are

no white guilt table of contents
hidden white privilege footnotes
how much commentary does it take
to build a career on our backs?

better to build a barricade of books
better than a sister or brother
telling lies like the big one

"not many Indians write, edit or
  publish their own books in Canada"

enough written enough to
       disgrace disrespect
              displace/replace/deface
the most obvious lie
it helps them
financially to help us poor Indians
help us out of a grant to publish
help us out of a teaching position
help us by editing us out
or in collusion
      white out our efforts
by helping us not write/publish/edit
     our own words culture history

someone might drown in the pity poor us
bust a gut when we beat off imitators
nobody has to be that sorry for us

let's not worry about being mean to them
we're going to be very busy
building a barricade
they won't know we mean business
they must see the barricade
they will have to send in the army

to stop us from reading our books

nevermind me

nevermind me say like
      nevermind me okay
            nevermind body essence
                  nevermind spirit presence

nevermind what I say
      nevermind what I do
      supposed to do what next
            nevermind me on the road
            why I came here in the first
                  nevermind place in society
                  never ever remind me again

nevermind anyone
      nevermind me especially if I obstruct interrupt
      respect honour obedience convenience of situation
      inclusion exclusion on the right side of same issue

nevermind rewind
      nevermind you drop subject never have time specifics
      wait for a spell put on protest privilege what the hey bale
      clear the air forked tongue opening address progress
        backward

nevermind for instance
      last nevermind me avoidance lone bystander braced for
        rejection
      perhaps a fax long email seven page letter detail of facts
        history
      political plather profound repentant stare at moccasin
        orthotic style shoes

Better Dressed

Indigenous colour wheel
depends on season shifts
you go white to the bone
in winter yet red in marrow
spring is very green crispy
twenty dollar bills budding
income tax rebate or long
awaited residential school
compensation but if casino
or bingo lucky you can bank

summer finds you lazier
mosquitoes love to bite
through your deep blue sleep
in fall you get rouged up
geese honk above you
gathering season switch
spirit flies upward to catch
higher altitude wind soar
magenta sundowns elevate
admit it don't you just hate
revelations of nature change

you are the one better dressed
ndn skin colour enhancer
outshine night auroras boogie
lifting big foot moccasins high

I think I know you way better
you were the poor bastard
pushed out in front of a store
you sold leather bikinis wolf
tail boas just another ndn
wearing fake turquoise beads

did you know that Running Bear
and Little White Dove sang out
for Kaw-liga to quit the cigar store
subterfuge of his bulging loin cloth
tomahawk loaded to educate
tourists with swift chop of wood?
he clubbed another tame tobacco
indulgent movie goer in early
mockumentry wooden he quit
stoicism take off exotic outfit?

doubt your baggy pants produce
you are just another poser hoser
ordering mooseburger with poutine
I am in line behind you at the stand
they can't run out of ndn traditional
diets I will hunt beefalo in freezer
ask if wild rice casserole available
you are just showing off your crack
boxers beat tidy whities wedged

want you to be real but me first
eh today eh yesterday okay eh
big party aboriginal you kept me up
last night with your one beer fight
your braids long enough tradish
you grew them yesterday I got
my cheque just for you and kids
mystery how old man incarcerated
keeps me available for next pow wow
pretend I am your lifelong snag

back burner

back burner

BACK BURNER

at the bookstore wild impulse
walk out with book and file folders
flagrant exit through the door
if stopped or apprehended
mumble a story
forgetful type
doesn't remember
what is held in hand
bungle job having been in past a prolific shoplifter. put all
that stuff over the years in the back of my mind. just another
backburner. a cauldron bubbles froth. witches brew or Red River
stew? hard to discern the taste from the nostril attack of the
aroma. each nostril hair is played like a fiddle. soon to be ready.
soon to be served.

this backburner cliché has to be vogue. just sit with yuppie
Starbuckites sipping. whenever asked about deadlines, give the
easy reply "it's on the backburner."

my life is on hold.

HONEST PIECE OF WRITING

so what? revelations about macho-inclined traditions? dare to
assume the macho came with the beliefs. perhaps. reinventions
of the sweat lodge and sweet grass smudging ceremonies sure
pushed us urban victims of traditional scams into the Indian Act.
we were supposed to be a disappearing act off the reserve. now
we are so spiritual and healed.

a lively discussion ensured. sounds like Minutes from my Last
Meeting with Other Gabby Females. the topic being bogus
medicine men. women excluded for some strange reason. who
healed who. too personal but have medicine women prayed

enough. as in P-R-E-Y on the men. do they predate the men as in predator. do deadly women need more compassion? the "my people" schlock grabs my gizzard. motion to adjourn anyone? did we discuss men who use the "medicine man" role to control women yet?

PRINCESS AVERSIONS AND DIVERSIONS

maybe writing memoirs is not such a good idea. tell all? discover my "princess" aversions. maybe my "princess" paranoia is about not learning what a woman has to do to become independent.

what is a "rez princess" anyway? naive? very much into mainstream marketed spirituality? she's candled her ears again! she pulled with all her pull. out popped Pocahontas and gang. right, she's got a gang now.

the other night in front of family, assorted friends and fiends brought up the subject of how much race hate was in the movie *Pocahontas*. didn't minimize. just said, "sorry, still race hate". no, it's not just the hour glass figure on the woman. focus on another part of the body. the head needs critical attention.

see a little girl watching *Pocahontas* movie to discover her "magic" just like her grandma watched Tiger Lily kidnapped by Captain Hook. are Pocahontas and Tiger Lily relatives? is there a Disney "Indian" intergenerational clan system?

heard Russell Means voice in contrast to his real life daughter talking disappointment in father figure. he needed the Disney movie to father a fantasy of fatherhood. even if father is a cartoon guy, he's worried his daughter "Pocahontas" acts a tom boy.

my dad wasn't a chief. he taught me to play baseball. helped me practise hitting then had to learn how to run bases. both Pocahontas and Tiger Lily were captives. was Tinkerbell accessory and collaborator or was Wendy prototype feminist fixer upper?

TOUGH TITTY

"tough titty" was a 50s saying hardly hear it ever said. now we have to be "nice Indians" and not "picky" or "too contrary". AIM guys were called "Assholes in Moccasins". don't have to be a member of the American Indian Movement to have anger judged as "unjustified".

maybe writing about the 60s is better. so nobody knew me as a radical. nobody was that radical to begin with. nobody was radical to me except for that priest in Milwaukee. he listened to my story. helped me escape helplessness for a moment.

now and then "too radical" is a tag someone puts on another person. think of the women who rode with White Bird. Nez Percé woman survived a gunshot wound. rode across the border her baby on her back. the border to Chief Joseph's people was a Medicine Line.

no medicine lie. nobody was that radical. except for an unknown woman with a name not forgotten. so many don't even know her name.

NOT THE NATIVE WAY

how hard it is for me to accept a person who lies about identity is because so many people lie. sick of the lies.

watching *North of 60* makes me wanna puke. can't help appreciate the polished concise scripts, the dialogue style ... so brutal ... no time for buildup. noticed how everyone goes for the jugular right away. seriously. seriously. Betty Noses says it that way. not much laughs for all the serious show.

SAFE POEM

climbed a flat iron mountain in Boulder, Colorado. start of the 90s and Oka decade. a poet made us go for a walk unlike all the others who just did the poems about nature from the safety of home.

mind you an execution happened that very summer on that same mountain. skinheads threw someone down. a guy died because he might've snitched but they got caught for killing him. unlikely these killers from Toronto. most likely Canadian violence gets more ugly in another country.

so used to it. Oka catches on around the country. no use to leave home to protect commonwealth. save a golf course for wealthy. remember people afraid of the "wilderness" what First Nations people called home. Canadian nature is more violent whenever recreation destroys creation.

CNN WITHOUT CABLE

my TV is now the back window. cattle outside in the field. CNN. Cow Nations News.

cow watching. falsely demeaned species. as soon as the hay truck got closer to them, the moo signals got regular. more rhythmic.

humans malign the hamburger bearer. cows were orderly beings. different moo calls on the way to the feeding station.

THE SCISSORS THAT KILLED SOMEONE

dad talked about the scissors when used to cut off loose threads. put buttons on his green work pants for suspenders to catch hold. he was a caretaker in a block. someone hid the scissors.

inherited the weapon when he died. scrubbed once with silver cleaner. still kept a dark grey look on the blades with rust brown blood shadow. held special scissors in hand, cut off tape on boxes to be shipped to B.C. feel the power as protection.

got to take the scissors to a witch or psychic fair to be read for more details.

FUNGUS AMONG US

told to get fungus that grows on the willow or is it birch tree?
purify house and also all sharp pointy objects. even sweet grass
the mail. good advice to protect a woman's art from exploitation.
protect self and space from intrusion.

existence a terrible mundane. each dustball on the floor shows
how unconnected an occupant is from immediate environment.
the script yet unwritten is evisceration. filing system nil for last
few years. not a question of "to file" or "not to file". it was "to
pile". piled up paper all over.

bad medicine is fear. once a frightening image came to me in a
sweat lodge. fear visualized. a troubled relationship. saw a small
figure that had to be an incubus. the terror of an idea made me
overreact. years later, the message is easily interpreted. a simple
dictionary definition deciphers incubus vision as "dead weight".

good medicine has to be looked up. fungus of the mind.

WRITING AUTHORITY

author tea unlike authority is whenever author lets it be known
who or what author is about over a cup of tea. imagine a group
of writers with duelling teapots to pour. each venue, workshop or
conference would serve tea. with or without ceremony.

BLAH BLAH BLACK SHEEP

blah blah black sheep writer, got any bull? yes sirree, keep
writing the same stuff over and over without rhyme reason.
better answer: yes mam or sir, just give a moment to mull. or is it
cull? null?

THIGH NOODLES

not Thai noodles. sensuous noodles fatter on one end than
another. passionate pasta, so sure.

cultural poverty of the urban rez is almost beyond description yet it's where much of respected work called art or literature gets produced.

try to find turf. defend the very polluted stale air. be on the land anyway to come on home. never be an orphan afraid of own family.

relative. all related. all relatives. all the ways. all the way. relate this. just relate. be related again. never too late later.

she breaks off

collaboration of split selves
talk to a woman in '76
skinny nervous wreck
in '91 not too late to meld our beings

am not together enough to grasp
fragment she wrote not knowing.
it would only be me
would read her words
decipher the meanings
only three days to tell me.

Day 1
starts with bureaucrats have no colour or race
the struggle would be for her individual person
she did not trust the elites because she was on
her way out of marriage university jobs galore
not the quick rabbit losing victory to the turtle
who plodded on in the fable to win over human race

she had stopped to reassess her life
she was taking a breather
got passed up though
others got the degrees
she did not reach academic goals
that one

not that big of a deal
Indians didn't have goals
that's what Clyde Warrior told her
when she asked if he ever had one
look forward
plot life on a chart
proceed

was not the Indian way
Indians dreamed

she had a dreamquest
but back in '71 she just wanted
to improve herself wanted to be
educated the clever con shot
gotta say we have to be educated
who wants to be taken for being
a "stupid" Indian or worse "ignorant savage"
"uncivilized" or be called the "stupid squaw"
she tried too hard not to be
overdid trying to be accepted by other standards

she still had her own ideas deep inside

her dream was an educational institute
designed by her and for her own self
call it the Sacajawea Foundation
contempt on the persons like Sacajawea
she helped the white colonizers
made her appear the martyred sister

by saving the name of Sacajawea
she would save her own destiny
she kept her colour and race by dropping out
a smart move
had to pay the price
she had little faith in herself
her self under siege

Day 2
she confessed that she needed counselling
content with housework always eased depression
imagining she had fun but the resident sick one
made her stop quit the hangover grieving lost soul
gang that one quit everything groovy to be with

she did not say she had tried to reunite with relatives
back to the rez fiasco didn't work give or take
all the drinking parties and assorted romantic flings
convinced her she did not belong to anyone or
country university marital status parent authority

she was only a fragment of who I ever was
maybe the one that held her back was me
don't know why I did it because she wasn't happy
it's not like I broke up a good thing if I was the one
she had to take care of me first but I had split off
from her delusions of grandeur so much trouble
I'm trying to figure it out why the inner squirrel died
inside that one huge compulsion to kill vicariously

Day 3
she got busy with self help program Indian AA group
it made her want to go back to street life brief as it was
in whatever shape she returned the pattern remained
she was a split up person but each and every analysis
would lend itself to hating the separations she was

on her list of childhood incidents she put first the alcoholism
of her mother and signs of severe mental illness
child molester had been second but second thoughts figured
out poor urban and mixed blood doomed figure portrayed
in born victim sequel of street theatre role she scripted

the plus side was the essential fact her mother was Indian
not ever to change in fact her mother disappeared long ago
even if she had to be more Indian because her mother was
no good drunk but caught up to her in the end hurting her

Day 4
never was written maybe she knew something inside her
spoke leaving only a faint track of what she had to do so
difficult to communicate with her messages left for me

wants me to talk for her explain why Woman of Colour
position for professor teaching about Aboriginal Feminism
did not pursue her and why follow up pension did not
materialize then what about a second, third, fourth chance
but maybe this is the place where I need to break off again

Succinct Savage Subtext

Sublime sin is subversive sloth.
Search for superlative transgression
is a waste of superb time and silly putty.
Contra dictation in speech spelled out.
Spirituality suckered back slow slug
style into shame stride so secret sacred.
Size of head dress indicates sad sly
sell out stance or chief Lies In His Face
or Pants colanders sick soul slime space.
Sensational sensing of scarred syllables.
Submit soon to sacrifice backslider sulk
yet loathe subtle wraparound remains
hardly suggest star burst satisfactions.

How many feathers in a warbonnet
tickle fancy vile verbal utter sputter?
Forked tongue forensics show off
self serving crock talk diplomacy.
Stay mum and numb first nations.
Stoic whisper campaigns sneak up.
Say it again. Shut up if you speak out.
Ask relevant questions to our flat ass
association but fine tune the fiddle
for after the big pow wow is over
we get advice to cry after apology
given for government genocide
sponsored residential schools.
Media scans ho hum responses
across the country waiting to put
a smile on subversive stone faces.

What ancestor carved a pictograph
in this eye to fight this syndrome?
Drone on until ancient song takeover.

Read between the lines for signs.
Massage that tomahawk gently
to further the fling of truth now
it brings out savage after glow.
Cheek pushes scowl past censor.
Undertones too high decibel.
Defiant war cries must re-echo
memories not that easy to forgive.
Shake the loose warbonnet loose.

Bloody Jig Why Ever Stop Fiddling Around

riel   riel

died   died

lie

didn't we

take our blood back

fan out shake rattle roll

one snare drum bang big drum

half white half chief half his people

half people jig have half the blood he had

we keep it riel give holiday tribute comeback

Road Signs Poem

Indian Blockade Ahead
Slow Down Or Else

Ignore White Man Road Sign
You Are In Indian Country

Star Truck
The Next Generation

Approaching
Bingo Palace And Casino
Speed Down

White Women Ahead
Watch Behind

Caution
CIA/CSIS Surveillance Zone

Flying Dust Reserve

Come To A Complete Stop
Throw Out Anchor

Coyote Crossing

Keep Your Eyes On The Road

Pot Hole Next

Pot Hole Again

Keep Right Jesuit Roast
Mohawk Special
Indian Summer Potluck

First Nations Men At Work
Forest Fire Again

Indian Reseratti Mechanic
First Drive By

Passing Lane
As If

Warning Don't Pick Up
Strangers
You Might Be Related

Road To Nowhere
Just Follow It
You'll See
You Are Now Leaving Rez
May The Rez Be With You

Last Ditch Religion

what about the Jesus picture in the house?
spirituality becomes a guessing game
have to call myself something believable
when visiting a rez

                    I am told about an elder
what he said to a person
not too sure of a church to join

he asked   what about after death
if body   gets thrown in a ditch

even the born again traditionals would be
buried in a church cemetery   when too late
to suggest a proper burial   because the right
righteous relatives want   that way

so I found a faith   won't spout evangelical

the spirits of the Mayans are back   so I might
testify to ancestors back in Mongolia   how I
know I am related to Pocahontas   I have been
both Asian & Indian in former lives   besides
being a drunk Danish sea captain killed in brawl

I neglect to talk hellish about the Catholics
& sexual abuse & Pentecostal cover ups &
how Christians murdered Jews

don't want to convert anyone by accident
if I could be a Mayan scribe   writing down
major events of the day   I would write
it all down in stone   rest assured
tribute to the belief in that last Ditch Indian

what is written on paper will dissolve decay
go back to the earth where more sacred a stay

Underskin

raised hand
a sign of peace
surrender

white black settler
newcomer buddy
admire

gentle stone stare
history written plaque
lies

foolish pose insult
snickering kids hate
history

walking in moccasins
never worn out
run

this generation never
speaks how killers
pacify

leather adornments
velvet beads fur
forewarn

radical goofy grin
apology wince bow
loosen

looking glass water
holds pathetic stance
escape

a gross takeover
going to steal a horse
yell

entwine fist in mane
crack in hoof
capture
me must jockey
pooped out future
steal

hotwalked showered
in carousel parade
trot

had won wont
spiritual vision
release

no use no business
back to the park
return

found exact spot
vigil for decades
fascinate

better eye kept
fellow spirit prison
possess

gets under skin
has no business
enter

use me temporary
transport trifle
trick

End Whale

Street kids in Regina wonder about a whale
what has this mammal business to do with
a fighter and an adopted Métis child who
hanged himself mixing up words is easy
he'd be alive now but I wouldn't want to be
in his place either as he was always moving
one foster place to place misplaced displaced

he became a fighter as far back as he would
remember except he would always remember
pain that time he got beat up wetting the bed
wouldn't mind to watch him win his next fight
shouldn't get knocked around no matter what
a kid does because caring adults responsible
should tell his worker while watching tv news

seems three California grey whales got trapped
in Arctic ice. Eskimo rather the Inuit chisels and
chain saws cut a string of 24 rectangular holes
stretched half a mile toward the open channel
day and night they worked to free mammals
a lot like humans but still the youngest one died

pretty neat how tough people around me been
there done that ramming their heads into walls
needed them the most against the ice inside me
poor whale might be alive today just endlessly
the need to share pain again and again hidden
legacy across generations mysteries get shared
below the ice society won't melt down sooner

granny boot camp

Gynegran

Double emphasis. Gynecratic. Gynecentric. A choice
to show what is a more common down to grandmother
earth way to tell what women elders or seniors might do.

Okay, too redundant? Gynecratic granny. Gynecentric.
Stubborn attachment? Where's the wisdom? Eccentric?
Plain old kokum, gaga, tupa, nokomis does not do justice?

Gynocracy was government devised by older women way
back when Spider Grandmother inspired Pueblo women.
Gone before us people told of a different governance system.

Basic grannydom. More than Princess for a day. Princess
plus is exaggerated claim. Priestess, Poetess, Prophetess,
Visionary and Seer. We must pump up that Geritol image.

Medicine Woman Not. She is the medsin alone gathering
power. Feminist Not. No complacent matriarchal vision.
More days off the rag gives women time for age reversal.

Let multivitamin kick in. Role model ourselves. Check
into the downtown health club as fat squaw exit slim svelte.
Throw cane away. Jump up out of the confines of scooter.

Jog in place. Join that Grandma parade with mall brats or
drag them to protest march. Introduce them to all relatives
not just the blood gene pool survivors we know all about.

I will proudly wear a button MEDICINE WOMAN NOT.
The fakery that passes for new age shamanism strikes us
credulous. On the bright side, it is similar to performance art.

What underlays human exterior was animal. Coyote chaos.
Accidents. Everything awry happens doesn't fit future plans.
Coyote is flexible and inconsistent. Adaptable contradiction.

Coyote starts something then changes mind right away.
Tricksters had to scheme a life. Way out of trouble. Think
quick to stay alive. Get out of the way conformity will crush.

Are tricksters those who resist? Do they need permission
for who they are? Are they colourful interesting people?
Won't follow goddess gospel? Keep on resisting resistance.

A colourful person is an animal stuck with bird feathers like
Ms. Coyote. Squawky birds had dive bombed her. In her
sweat lodge she howled and yelped out soothing tunes for aches.

Her ceremony with dancing leg covered in feathers worked.
I search for sanctuary where grandmothers and grandchildren
are respected and celebrate visions of generational veneration.

CY-BRO-GRAN-MOC

MUDer She Wrote: Risky business for
Cyber Granny or Elder to become
disoriented upon entering a MUD room.
What is she supposed to say? Is Tiny
Pow Wow a bit too much?

Went down like dis: Cyber Gran says
"let's party!" Cyber Warrior counters:
"party rrr." Cyber Granny gets back:
"party smarty."

Cyber Coyote closes: "party harty'er?"
Cyber Gran advances: "coyote why
I hardly."

Cyber Warrior demands: "braid my
hair." Cyber Gran continues: "up
braid yourself."

Cyber Coyote intrudes: "party animal?
Ya talking to me?"
Cyber Gran utters: "Aaiiaaii."

Cyber Warrior inquires: "was dat a
mating call?" Cyber Gran disses:
"why are you Métis?"

Cyber Coyote chants: "doing it doing
it why I hardly." Cyber Gran: "ever!"

Cyber Coyote tops off: "ever-e-ver."

Cyber Warrior enlightens: "best to
catch on early. people in Cyber

Tipi room creep on all fours then
switch genders!"

Cyber Gran ejaculates: "right after
bannock and tea, heya hey." Cyber
Coyote after plays: "braid my tail."
Cyber Gran posts: "got ugh?"

Happy trails entwine. Couple of
coyotes get together in Cyber Tipi.
Couple years after too many coyotes
for one tipi. Cyber Warrior fends off
Cyber Gran hands tied. Wow! Cyber
Warrior braids own hair gender free.
Cyber Gran texts: "Ugh Me Already."

Granny Ear Rot Tick

Itchy ear. Cotton swab makes it worse. Tingle sensation.
She was total turquoise not off colour comedienne or blue.
Not a Prairie Chicken Lady with a fowl tongue was she.

She did not attend a residential school run by the Grey Nuns.
They had dirty habits that shocked even her mind set.

She was one to defend the Long Stranger particular Tonto
not real homo sapiens because Silver got raped constantly.
PETA — People for the Erotic Treatment of Animals said so.

She was on the Fatkins Diet. Grannyaholic addiction.
Survivor of Granny Boot Camp. She offed the inner nun.
She was called "cochon" or "sauvage" by sleazy sisters.
"Awass" she told them "Go back to the Virgin Islands."

She did not follow her man whenever he showed up.
Would not guide him by walking in front and signalling.
In a good mood, she would walk beside her partner but
nevermind side back or front she would walk all over him!
Lust for an anthropologist had her pow wow on his face!

She attended a karate course when she worked as caregiver.
The worst part of the job was the old men groping her.
She had already been approached by elders when young.
She watched TV commercials for Viagra testimonials.
Guys learned how to dip dance and perform foreplays.

Her confidence was lucky even with grey snatch hairs
and a 90 year old vagina she would still be sensitive to touch.
She would not fear being bald in her private parts
obvious was grass did not grow on her race track that much.

End of the trail drama did not disturb her one bit. She did listen just once to a great horny owl that called her names. "You old fat bitch." She was not fazed out by that talk.

Her Erection

Chosen to be erect. Stand up straight.
Her want simple to be upright righteous.
Outside flagpole stands erect unlike her.
If raised right she'd be bristling beautified.
Why again cat faced the dog with fur erect.
Extra huge fur tail wave scared him off good.
He returned the next day to complete installation.
Lovely couple set up television antenna on roof.
Simple polish of the knob brought in more channels.
Need be not erected on a firm base independent alone.
Woman totem pole wrecked years ago in stellar cellar.
When the missing parts arrived he inflated her desire.

Hanging Poem

bother on the phone hang up let go
surveillance daddy-o tail hanging
outside pantses leave me alone ask me
I was a good Indian today hanging
around whites do-gooders rich people
hanging by own hangnail no dangle
little pinkie yo yo pull compulsion
strange hanging jaws makes tongue
hang gaga only hangup you gape much
hanging tough hanging fast around
blow with the wind stay on washline
winter rigid shapes merge mania
dry out treatment withdrawal transfix

retreat into nightmare

spun twist of braid
cavity brain used to be
girl corpse
half buried in a moss surrounded hole
bark dress was torn from the waist up
she remains a stump

brown shoes on island path
he stopped by tree
resting position disturbed
bush skirt pulled off
inescapable hurry

she was a tree who speaks
story existence by the pond
ghosts come to haunt present
no one in particular cares
a murder happened hundred years
mystery dream killer
I wear brown shoes

pond will not cop
shoes wade water edge
fill up to gush out
broadcast news

lone male goose resident
had no partner
female duck dropped by
built nest and laid eggs
goose became surrogate father

drake feathers remain
close to path around pond

brown frog jumps out
pauses to let me examine
spotted back I admire

special find is storytelling
diamond shape rock
points in two directions
surface is rust ochre
rock screen shows small bear
mallard feathers float down
deep inside the stone
eagle flies beak full of baby otter
women dance through the stone
frog swims shedding rust brown coat
underside the rock are tipis
or perhaps fossil leaves
imprint the story
back in a city apartment
woman artist makes another
Elvis Presley impersonator
dream catcher

next to my brown shoes
are horse tails
eldest plants on the island
under the tree shade
dead stumps in silence
brown shoes
took the trees away
planted surrogate

brown frog feet
swim circles in pond
otters are making a comeback
brown paws walk by Otter Pond

Forget Grandmother

Woke up one morning to forget new status as grandmother
cognizant barely I am a woman of nature listen up now girl
nature is saying I understand everything I forgot grandmother
chance culture shows me not too certain over not knowing
what to do each morning the quick little steps warn me I must
pretend grandmother she asks again "coo coo, where are you?"
pays to answer or she might colour a design on me with marker
like she did yesterday when I accidentally posed as a toy or doll

Hardly Any Direction

egg ran between fingers
align yoke no joke way
way too slippery to grasp
private kumquat left debris

last night foresee naked
survivor of fifteen household
changes in less than a decade
2 and a half tons of junk pile
climate change won't rearrange
took lotta lumps in the 50s too

baby picture is smiling Buddha
in drag with lace bonnet and frilly
lace dress squint eyed laughing

Black Thread Around

hard stare at an Inuit carving
      shaman pose with black
          thread tied to tooth
strong yank
          suspended animation
one look in a mirror after clean jerk
troubling tooth extraction
      shows vacancy
      tentative tongue
      explored cavity
then I was just a kid
toothless being temporary
heartless faceless disability
commands if the eye offends
pluck it out of body or mind
      throb bleed ache
      disfigure disorient
      cause more trouble
who is to blame for residual
      anguish hysteria
      anxiety angst?

should a shaman snare
whip off offensive visage
wriggling smiles half
apology aided abetted
wrinkles scowls frowns
forehead lined furrows
prefer cosmetic surgery
a botox fill in lieu of face
pulled off by black thread
shamanic string continues
captures angina symptom
removal tug heart immediate

preventive actions not taken
      could not repair it
      in time had to face
give up on compassionate
self care but not right way
slow last murmur to beep
flatline wait for final thump
as if turtle heart devoured
in youth would prevent onset
deadly lonesome heart beat

Lady Earth Diver

Years ago. Moons past. Lady Earth Diver jumped up.
Her sleek body twisted and turned in the air. She
dropped. Paws pointed to the surface of the water that was
everywhere at this time. She hit the water in a nosedive.
Then she slid under the waves. The water beings must
have known she would hit bottom.

She would sink with her paw extended. Then with a slight
stroke upon the mud below, she swam back up toward the
light. Water squeezed her sides. Water squeegeed out
of her. Her last gasp for air she made at the surface.

She floated helpless but in her mind was the prayer. Make
a world from what is in my paw. It should be enough
for a small mud pie. It's not that much. On Turtle's back, this
gift will grow.

My child memory convinces me that I spoke my mother
language, Ojibwe, with my mother. I remember always
hearing the sing song speak of my aunties and cousins as
they worked in the house. My father spoke English and
so I no doubt experienced a bilingual upbringing until my
mother disappeared. Then I learned silence. That loss must
be close to what linguists refer to as the end of mother
tongue fluency in a person especially a child. Did I feel
numbness? Did my breath stop as it does in near
drowning?

Best Corn Soup Ever Tasted

She brings me blue corn soup
to heal us both where it hurts
the hearts of men and us most
blue corn works sure recovery

So I sat there bruised black and blue
in L.A. cockroach city apartment
this guy with fist to my face
when not choking throat
hers too was bad she said
her words proof I was not alone

Corn was ancient woman
she gave flesh spirit
tassled corn grandmother
brings woman nation together

ever good corn soup tasted
Kahnawake pow wow was true
Mohawk clan mother harvest

Chinese recipe calls for special
fetal corn with sweet broth
alternative blessing time it takes

precious survival makes me older
wizen enough to remove husks
boiled cobs dry on mesh frame

time comes for me to cook up
pot of corn soup thrown on stove
treatment for intergenerational trauma
this corn concoction ensures life span

as if one bear

as if one bear

tempted to make a small stuffed black bear replica
                              gaudy girdle of feathers
                              around waist every colour
                              use a button for the eye
except modest embellishment of a thin curved red
arrow spirit line through his torso more humble a project
saw such a brooch at an art gallery store summers back
too expensive too much coin for a senior to spare

a party invitation would stimulate creating the bear fetish
          with a wild polka dot dress up suit
          not only would I trash my heritage
          give approval
          adorn protection
          display consumer spirituality

with protective talisman I better ward off trauma

suspend decisions
                    bare breast my feelings
                    or sport this trendy trophy
debate outcomes
                    favourable for instant group therapy

free interpretations of my medsin might cure onlookers
control intermittent unknown fears for the curious

engage beneficial conversation by stating I am quite proud
my inner terror yet fears about men caution me not to brag
as small occasion it is to exhibit celebrate realistic fears
disability might be a mixed blessing over and above survival
expressed gratitude must be the greatest condolence cure ever

          entitled to the residual fears earned

privileged to retell abuse litany
forego advice: mustn't point finger or name predators

bear images are essential to inner call for familiar guardian
given courage never had when first threat showed ugly face

understand what I felt wasn't only one fear
therapists or counsellors guide past insight
flash fear of violence also opposite such fear
gathering my own precious bundle of power
temporarily knock self out of a balance with surge
what used to be uneasiness around men likely momentary
adjustment between feeling confident and slipping back
chronic shyness
stare down at toes blink

awkward unresolved rage toward all men because of past
trauma makes me hateful man hater I say I am not close
first memory of death in still sleepy eyes goes far back
mother is dragging me by the arm middle of the night
we run up to a policeman and she tells him about berserk
whiteman landlord chasing us with butcher knife
three or four years old when racial incident takes
away restful sleep options
layered memories accrue

how a simple bear fetish won't always remove the dread

need a stronger medsin to blur the fright of sober husband
at the time attempt to ram the hunting rifle under my chin
forced away was a murder
inside wreck fought to hold
back the barrel point it up
ceiling light over our heads

wasn't too damn exceptional
replay and replay and replay
thoughts of never retribution

foreground of monotonous activities
skeletal body weight 116 pounds
losing steady interest in life death
endurance await the next beating
accept pain and suffering of others
more apologetic starving and helpless
woman will not let the murder plot
unfold even as aggressor bears down
she counters bears up bears with
knock out champion four bears blow

as if one bear when bear clan intervenes

south dakota news

The *Argus Leader* in Sioux Falls printed
news years ago about militants. Today
Indian people no longer blame anyone but
themselves. No matter how you treat them
it is the other guy gets the breaks in the news.

    South Dakota to South Africa
    a long road to walk
    Mississippi of the North

    arrest Indians
    not city businessmen
    damned embarrassing
    walking around
    drunk Indians
    nuisance

    get them out of society
    individuals not Indians
    50 years integrated
    after all it makes sense

You stand over a dead cow in the middle of the
road on a checkerboard reservation. Only one
side is tribal. The rest go by blanket rules.

You line up all the Indians to sentence them.
Whites go one by one. Only 10 percent of the
population of South Dakota make up 20 percent
of the arrests. Nothing new in the news.

    next generation will be worse
    young men and women grow up
    never being punished

Indians lack ambition
carry a chip on their shoulder
when if you see them walking
on the road gravel paved or ruts

Whites drink in private bars in their own
neighbourhoods. Indians can't afford to
drink in the nice bars, you see them on
the street. You invent more stories.
They are people without a home unwelcome
even on the reservation or border towns.

It's insulting then to say "go home".
You know all the answers even to that one.
If you can't beat them up, join them for
a drink. Spread your kind messages.
Indians must become white to succeed.
A reservation is a perfect place for crime.

Different mantra: Whites must become Indian
to fully understand. Make Elvis Presley chief.
One warbonnet he deserved for flaming star.
Elvis was blood brother. Part Cherokee.
You put any group of whites on a reservation,
they'd do the same. Shaky at first.

    sweat lodge
    pray sister pray
    for a better way
    our flag is frayed

It's a cop out to say that two whitemen
killed an Indian woman and spent 3 months
in jail. The cops went out for coffee excuse.

Wasichu paper doesn't get all the news.

    walking on the right side

of the road
sun going down
they hit me

It reports that these people live in violence.
If you do something violent to them, it doesn't
hurt them nearly as much.

uncertain it was human
might have been some garbage
maybe she was lying
on the road

More Indian cars are stopped. Never pick up
white drunk ranchers. No one spends a day in
jail. For first degree manslaughter, you get
a suspended sentence. An Indian was killed.

remember Chief Eagle
he was cold and hungry
he got 5 years
stole that can
hot dogs & beans
from a parked car
on Main Street

You have to hire people that don't fit the image
of Indian so they can see cops as people. They
are harder on their own kind.

pour the wine on the ground Chief
turn the bottle upside down
let me pour you a drink
inside your pocket
let's put this one
in a dumpster
check on him later

White people fear Red people on the front page.

lonely stretch of highway
patrolman pulled this Indian over
tell me I'm a racist
put me on the defence
I am asking for it

multicultural timbit

Suspense at airport stopover. I walk back and forth to exercise. Cannot find a Timmies. Wonder what country I am in. Just Toronto. Then I see a star descending from the heavens via plane. He is a stellar presence in a First Nations universe. He's an actor so he gives me a tip on how to pretend to speak French by adopting a fake accent and drooping a lip à la Chrétien. Shrug often too. I am on the way to Quebec and must bust through the language barrier. I know the word "poutine" so I will not starve for sure.

The flight attendant on the plane does not give out a *Globe and Mail* to me. Did she figure out I was "anglais" and "autochuck"? To her, I might be part Métisse but do not speak Michif. If I spoke in hand signals, the message that I want a Tim Horton donut might be mistaken for a terrorist threat. She might think I was suggesting a hole in the fuselage. Les amis pourquoi enough. I must learn to speak more French right away. How would I ask for a timbit? Do Canadian frequent flyers get their frequent fast food? I am starving.

On deese planes there is no room. Dis plane is so small for the fat ass or is that gross derrière. On the other plane I actually removed my shoes. Now I will have to say Excusez moi but I won't be able to add a reason. My feet get hot before the rest of me gets turned on. I will have to get into a yoga posture to tie my running shoe. Sacré bleu.

Un peu too! Wow, I am speaking Français. My adviser said to say "un peu" a lot. It means "just tiny". Miniscule, right? It would not help me to always talk this way. What if I met a well hung savoir faire dude? I must use discretion.

Always I get the wing on the plane. Like at a turkey dinner, I get to savour the part that might be used for soup. Aha! Has dis turkey been basted for instance as I do not want to get pregnant accidentally, eh? Excusez moi. I was thinking too much in

Anglais and it might be rude to explain all dis anxiety in another language barely taught in high school.

This plane will take hours plus of butt crammed into a crevice called a seat. My cheeks are to be pressured all the trip so they will become multicoloured. Multiculture maybe. I want a snack and dream of flying on an Aboriginal run hairline. I would get a baloney sandwich as a food preference. Ask for it by name. Tube Steak, please.

Maybe I am starting to speak broken Michif? I am broke usually. Oui, my blood has been thinned not by the injected semen of a known or unknown donor. No turkey baster or Petri dish for me. My dad gave away sturdy sperm cells which travelled the rugged canal to my mother's womb to decide my fate. Now that was a dangerous trip. Birthing was a tight squeeze as I weighed 13 pounds.

Need to travel more in Canada so I do not cling to the memory of the nearest Timmies. I need to be a bit more comfortable multicultural when I do.

Wooden Dance Fancy

Bin too busy bee me to attend da heritage Canada meet. Da glitter gleam hangout for dey conference Hindins. Never to jig der. Podiatrist says one foot cradle in da womb not ever pull out straight. Eben me know dat da tikinagan is outside da body altogedder so da defect did not 'appen der. Haff deformed foot. Wooden dance kick heel high at 'eritage pow wow. Dis back is no good hennyway.

Hindins not shy. Dey imitate Hollywood Hindin suppose dance in movies. Da udder Hindin people for strange reason wooden pud da hands on forehead to cover da heyes. Dat was before dey had sunglasses. Dey jump up an down like dey haff go toilet. Dey give 'oot an 'oller now an den. Oorons dance dis way. Udders wooden dance like dat.

Oh, da culture minister she please. Hindin friends dance for her and money. Dey circle one an udders. Dat big chuckwagon she keeps gubbermint money. She bait to mek Hindins settle down an stop da complain dey want act up. No more protest just dance fancy.

She lock heyes on big Hindin. Famous guy too. She wears Hindin gifts. Ribbon shirt an new mocs. He pick her to dance. She lift da harm so he grab harm to hold.

Less bless me. Mebbe I haff just haff culture an haff heritage. Dis too haff hass for dis multiculture behind. Bloomers fall down flat hass hennyway.

Knowhow

Know how want to know when even how was it for you?
Ask Jose. Not to be nosy. Just upfront. Before it happens.
For a snag he must admit he is Indio or Mayan. Damn it.
He is a white man in brown skin. Conquistador. Pretends
to know her. Sneaks up in Safeway. Alone in the aisle.

She attracted this mistake of identity. Saw a big party of
Native people exit house one day at noon. Trailing them
was a Central American dude wearing a toque with different
coloured yarns. He jumped in the cab with them to go to the
next pub party. Find schemes of refried love. Throw a chili
pepper into action. This Jose was popular. Stood by her now.

Drink to be somebody with him. Invite him to be ndn.
Strange, he did not ask her. "Do you mind dancing with
a man with an erection?" She had been walking around
with a large expensive cucumber in her hand. Turned
him on so he let her use his basket to hold the vegetable.
So she got academic. Spoke about her archeology class.
Maybe he was Aztec, Toltec, Inca or any kind Indigenous?

Too vague. Suspect. Undercover cop determined to
go undercovers with her. Her chance to expose creds.
She got it right. She cuddled that hard on with her thigh.
Slow danced. Held the trembler close tight damp delight.

first time I never lied

if it was medication talking
dare I often express viewpoint
deflect hand pinched throat
inhabit controversial space
I argue against immediate death
may take up impossible position
anti depress tongue in chat
stop passive insane response
panic cry eyes out feel sorry
crush pathetic self debates
useless points idle away hours

lie body down again sombre
reality returns get back edge
very mellow patient parasite
pharmaceutical conspiracy may
reconfigure a world afloat
full flagrant of constant bitch
polar ice cap melted down
polar bears washed up ashore
unable to surf global survival

when I never lied rarely
trouble spoke as lesser mind
I chose diplomatic words
gibberish jargon idiom
parlance dialect drivel
faced up to all alone put up
glare shut up stare defiance
put people in tell off place
shot careful at knee caps
disturbed and/or upset others
I quit buggy busy bee buzz
nectar full smile then supposed

sting of unwanted critical ideas
perforce patter to prevent lunge
fisted flick toward my person
I numbed out objective stance
engaged in less intense harangue
assumed another dialectic style

Rangutan Rage Writer

She makes it all up. She who knows me. She splits and makes up the stories in my absence. She saw me hide all night in a library. Saw the jealous husband chase me. She will look at me as I lug books to bed. I hide behind the text I read. Her eyes reflect me sawed in half. Says a magician took the other part. What is left is for a medicine woman to define. Our mothers are inside us anyway and might help us out even if they left us alone quite often. For men. For drinks. For laughs. Some of the mamas are popular aunties we visit for bannock and tea. They will become Old Ones. Keep us company. Respect our wounds. Sure got remedies. Pretty preachy words. They call each other a warrior but I don't know because I am only a sole survivor when nobody was around to defend me.

She watches me croon to the dance drum. Her focus on how I beat on Rangutan chest. Beat memories uncomfortable down inside the breasts. I keep forgetting so I compact it all. She is not that proud so she bears my wounds. She reaches for the trauma but manages to moan how the stab didn't quite do her in. She's so lucky for that gift. She is a buddy to my body. She was the one that wore the black eye. She coughed for me at work when I almost passed out from broken rib. She will convince me that I am angry for nothing. She accepted the abuse for me. I got nothing to talk about. She does keep it all straight. She does not always write it down like a police investigation. I must have to be ready for her to break the awful news to me. Yet many people attribute her anger to me and confuse me to hell.

Windigo Word Feast

what am I doing here as I look around I see I must be the fattest
one in a crowd of skinniest windigos I ever saw gathered at this
feast where I am to watch them devour words made flesh not
actual people every two years they meet so why not four well
it's government funded heritage so perhaps they might have it
every year but maybe they are on a strict diet & gather only on
occasion to gorge or go to binge heaven not too puritanical either
I notice as it is not a thanksgiving event because they start off
their menu agenda with appetizers best suited for dessert but
it is to tempt everyone to have sex even without a partner just
to show mind over erotica yet the big ogema windigo wiggles
his butt & thrusts his hips out to demonstrate how hot words
sound then keeps saying "eat me" as if he is the tasty tidbit
& not the words he is consuming well I never thought about
eating a windigo as I worried they were actual cannibals & this
advertisement about a word feast was to catch us off guard if we
wandered too close as they dined it is an upset to my stomach &
belief system as I did not know they were now taking words out
of ndn heads easy like a Hollywood cannibal might carve out a
brain from an exposed cranium & offer pieces of it to a person
to sample own thoughts but without knowing where actual
words originate at snack time or during a flight because now the
airlines offer so little food

Come Out From Behind the Yam

Scary guy is waiting to catch me again
if not paying attention to his moves.
He grabbed me to make me embarrassed.
I yell what do you think you are doing
as if I don't know he is a predator. I
mis-spoke to him at the bus stop. He
mis-communicated a single mis-action.

Later on I tell how he green ski jacket
black hair sweaty face put his hand
grabbed me made me think about him
get out of here you followed me. He got
brave enough to go underground after
me stepping off escalator at the mall.
In public he attacked victim waistline
because shopping crowd small like
he was short too maybe I was too tall.
He brushed against me but left bruise.

I am stuck somewhere psychology
does not map just a drop off location in
the mind. What if he jumps up
from behind again or finds me moving
to a new safe place crawls in behind
the TV set then jumps out when I go
to bed. Just think I am not safe
from him because he might be you. Tries
hiding in the cat pan but it's not that
therapeutic to guess whereabouts.

Maybe I won't throw you out because
I saw you in the vegetable drawer in the
fridge behind the yam. Then again I
might mistake your green jacket for that
old head of cabbage going bad. Pay
attention even after the fact helps me.

Weasel Woman waits

Seattle bus depot unexpected wait
weight inside festering gloom doom
avoid escalation of shouting argument
over money I don't have won't have

so implode make a quick exit before
I murder self dignity more than once
how many personal massacres does
it take to make last noble stoic stand

even Custer knew agony did he extol
get it over with redskins while arrows
whizzed past his quizzical head dodge
as I preach we have to stand in one place
with foot nailed down circle the mess

four long hours to wait for greyhound
bus depot looks scarier than hell bound
people look tough out the door the street
swarm no street charm after midnight

obsess many the times relive all faults
failed communication caused awkward
pause reset urgent emotional distance
necessary separation among loved ones

I now play the typical unpredictable brat
needy and too proud to cry hurt inside
then I notice the women who must travel
by night with kids some without suitcases
just boxes then I begin to associate escape
one night in a bus depot how I stood guard
with my son the toddler sleeping on a floor
he turns himself over to roll off the blanket

I could use truth and reconciliation to figure
how I now shape shift into a weasel woman
shifty in glance relentless swirl of poverty
life's strange tragedy is unknown conniving
weasel whose outer limits will always wait

Shards

smart women figure out what is important
dangerous & unusual to be a smart woman
she studied anthropology
      a science of broken pots
      & cultures that will die
she wanted to take the Maria Martinez pot
to show the class but it cost thirty thousand
she could not be trusted to handle to carry
valuable artifacts kept safe from appraisal
she was smart so she asked smart Pueblo woman
who knew other Pueblo women created the pots
thrown against walls to set the woman spirit free
      girl child saw the shards gather in pile
      archaeologists trouble themselves to dig
size & weigh each shard not knowing
different value for the woman being held
in broken pots was related to Woman
Who Thinks Us As We Are Being
missing pieces of the men's artifice puzzle debris
thoughts of domination revenge for being smart
women engineering students become hated targets
in Montréal they are executed in just another type
conversational casual encounter where smart women
get shot down in December '89 perverse put down
crazy associations calm feminist disassociation
each shard connects all women universal fight
each memorial brings us closer to sacred shard

commie conversations

tree bark reader

meanwhile back at La Quena
Walrus reads his paper
on the back porch
big news progressive change
set out early to meet up with
socialist writing group but find
no disappointment because

he transforms into a writer's writer
an encyclopedia of 60s who's who
his papers spread out on table
easily convince me of the great
social value of this eco project
how rain forest days pass slowly
removing tree bark determines
indigenous habitation land use

he lives in a wet tent year round
with slug and reusable bush
abundant with magic mushrooms
the fascination of how work shows
art doesn't need to kill the spirit
uncommon tale how white guy
fits into the native environment

a carver would remove a mask
from a tree and not kill creation
now once removed the artifact
might be stolen to museums
land animals plants people
essentials left alive to self sustain

this story didn't employ a carpenter
to witness an oyster easily bedazzled
or verify cabbages are rolls of dollar bill
offerings given to colonial riff raff kings

bin diver art

bin dive bin down bin up bin crazy easy days easy to say dazed
gutter thought utter rot snot what livid crash thru barrier reef
fathoms deep by whale lounge octopus sofa eel peeks shudder
rudder fin fish freak tank must leak sponge carnivore computes
escape swim west young flounder kick flick feet go distance raise
up then quick under waves sudden surprise fishy endings down
by the beach watermelons grow

devoid family pill works neck jerks forward backward spine
tingles arch back brain chemicals splash froth trough only a
synapse ago wanted good girls earn crummy jobs guys dissolved
in liquid orgasm vaginal canals surf up total shaft spoken for
good tight fit sheik vagina slow undiluted movement prevents
contraptions convoluted messages

grant award writers scheme dream queries understand process
why not poetic licences yes yes your slyness poet burns to
ash exits smoke stack smoulders in underpants potential
reproduction government

strain excellence defiance demands conditions crane levitate
taste tongue laps scraps teeth clench air word flow constricts
boa conductor grab onto metaphor crank light up furnace match
opportune window shuts up wad fuck up wad damn commic
grim plot steal money filter narrative drive

A Bit More Bukowski

& now the great Buck Owch Sky
will read a dare devil exploit poem
too gory so he cokes up can't finish
what he started to say was testimonial
blood filled the cracks of pavement
down Main Street outside busy pubs
for strange reasons I want to crack up
wasn't there that night I laugh it off
because in the future present tense I will
be glad he quit in middle of his Indian Act
he was doing good & on a roll so gutsy
he didn't smoke up either not much reefer
to stop from seeing another shank coming
more bleeding on the printed page to go on
his vigil he wanders absented minded by
guy sprawled on the divider broad daylight
flowers around him not cadaver chalk outline
he's just another passed out victim of atrocity
cars pass by either side and he's not that dead
to the world just Main Street Indian monstrosity
who does funeral rehearsal regular punch clock
blood remains in his veins for an entire library
collection Buck Owch Sky won't write down
way overwritten frenetic Red River Jig musical
take a break signal during show times customary
drunk ladies show off extra beer gut belly jiggle

december multiple haiku

help us feed our tropical
memory jungles

whoever else is
in the conversation it's
oneself one talks to

self-portrait sends out
what is wanted to be seen
pretending presence

clocks find tomorrow
rain rivers outside
muscular minding

rain bestows upon
us the way to another
washed off vancouver

rather than rushing
to anyplace else hurry
up to where we are

once upon a place
the wet footprints tamely dry
to smiles on wild's face

for gerry gilbert

Rev Me Up Double Take

In Nicaragua, a woman revolutionary celebrates
with her cadres. One of them might notice her
dark colour. Ask her if she has been to the beach.
It is a subversive way to ask if she is an Indian.
Stories told about solidarity & racism in Nicaragua
divulge greater quandary of how colour & class mix.
Woman thinks she must be Inca. Let's hope she is that.
She confesses she has many resemblances to one.
Cuna might be another possible rival ancestry.
For sure Cuna because she is so like a friend I know
who is genuine San Blas Cuna when dressed in regalia.

It is not always the convincing evidence we need.
Someone at work told her she has the hands of
a potter. Generations sculpted those hands. Proof.
Five hundred years have faded our recollections
of who we are. In 1992, we trade past glimpses.

I remember I am a Mohican queen not half
wit half baked half hearted descendant but one
total regal caste in blood bones bare chested
Indigena who paddled out to check her weir.
Never precious Pocahontas or Matoaka waiting
for discovery in original Tsenacomoco land.
Takes five centuries for resurgence take back
ancestral dreamtime before us forgotten women
use imperialist nostalgia to reconnect the power:

resistance revitalization regeneration revolt

Taken for granted a woman juggles identities
poet, revolutionary, Indian, mother, daughter
wife, ex-wife, grandmother & cultural worker
I catch a peek of who I am when she talks.

every bit race shell

do want to escape
slug it out without a shell
shell me dance shell she dance
shell we dance oo wee oo wee
shell fish one buys her product

shell wedge her body in twine
she space shell switch more wine
shell game race shell score
kick off watch her take off
she must be space shell lady crime
rough husk drops back to earth
lands on the dirt cover shell back
husky bitch turtle what becomes
dandylion crick neck captivates
where the shell used attached before

never race intended slurry under
pig trotters slippage on sludge
sea shells sea whore sell shells
race shell mix not worthy pressure
contents spread dicey wicey on table
purse open an um biblical sow ear
sea urchins secret untimely news
plenty pricks great porcupine head
porcine probable shell cases course
rack it up to racial unknowns
bi racial multi racial blown jobs
know what is talk about gross
dismember bent meant went vent

hardly an oink was heard above
hard hearing underneath each harley roar
extra space shell why not every

scream might blow out eardrum muff
higher pitch than a siren girl song
held to the ear meat mollusk moans
how space shell again space shell
shell the race begin or end period
bloody biz arterial blood fissure
that huge sow stands to hide behind

block clear view to a tiny piglet
pinch tale caught up in pubic drama
throats not choked combine each grunt

wow find unique condition all shell
except shun shell all face shell
said race shell business shell gain

Mind the War

Mindfield filled with visions not mine. Helicopters
whir. Bradley tank scoots quick to the right brain
after a shoot up at left ventricle. Protruding barrel
needle is just an oops excuse me accidental war.
Bilateral damage. Quick pick me up available at the
bipolar kiosk on the way down from sorry bout that
sand dune scatter. Look to the ridge. Hollywood
Indians line up. Whoop it up and please de-scalp
this time. Take off little to the left as usual direction
winds blow out. Wind up. Wind down. Wind
across fissures. Poof off the invasive force aka
enemy. Easy on the force, bro. Meanwhile back
at the synapse flood of serotonin occupies brain
terrain. Not to worry hey there's a meeting down
at the ganglia tonight. Show down at Hokahey
Corral. Back to circle one. Circle chuckwagons
but let's hang on tight to mounts. Hate to fall off.
Show medsin path plateau in case mind kill happens.

Duck Tape

Duck tape your duck
It might go to war
Tape your rubber plastic ducky
Together with a rubber
Two for duck feet
Then head out
For the Middle East
Your duck loaded
Duck!
All flying objects
Used rubbers
Shrink wrap
No tape a duck
A live one quacking
Pinch it by the tailfeathers
Make it quack loud enough
Videotape your rubber ducky
Set the duck afloat
Let it go with the current
Duck tape the mouth
Mind of American media
Canada could duck tape itself
Out of the war
Into the rubber ducky zone
How absolutely ducky!

Mama Sasquatch

ndn bag lady panhandling for a drink
interrogation reveals her a teacher
first friend during depression episode
I stare back at much ado sidewalk café
customers not even wanting a latte
Commercial Drive repels me lonely
need a job so I wander back forth
she became a true cement ndn type
teacher education did not prepare us
for street survival and her ass print
on the bench front of the bank is gone
was temporary sign of her presence
squeegee kids force her from corner
favourite bench taken away by bank
discouragement if we congregate
I witness her and she witnesses me
she understands I am poor in spirit
I teach poetry if given a chance but
she handed out bus tickets and took
me for Belgian fries to cheer me
Chinese wine will ruin her eyes
interfere with ministry to the boys
in her gang by Grandview Park
one dead body is found so bushes
cut back reveal bannock crumbs
she took boys home to clean up
only got more heavy eviction threats
housing so strict street people
give recognition of occupied
ndn territory as non natives notice
displacement of white guilt easier
give thanks for permission to shop
steal land base dominate new comers
if we go back time immemorial

greet ingratitude with goodbye
bag lady buddy is warning to me
next time I displace creative
writing instructor I will practise
Indigenous scribble on the cement
face Mama Sasquatch reflects to me

Commie Conversations on Commercial Drive

1. mountain coyote lights

Grouse Mountain lights up ski run
but Lucy in the Sky Diamonds guide
personal lope down The Drive below
better morph into witness of alternative
uncanny coyotes reception reflection
scenic outline from Burnaby approach
lights a shape shift of shark in the dark
neon cannot compete with these signs
street action interaction just compliment

substances abuse or choose lonely lust
get higher than the mountain coyote glow
how much dope does it take to take over
become the legend chicken duplicate
share an occasional escape or alley hideaway
daytime seagulls and eagles circle over the spot
by the Chicken Holocaust smell on Hastings
safer score when fancy mountain lights turn on

2. happy bear alignment

nobody believes this business name
easy to configure an image of bear nipples
okay the commercial aspect is fixing cars
but without preference for six breast bumps
there goes a need to be desperately fixated
won't pass up the offer two for right now
two for later use and two for lover friend
so the sign might indicate a chiropractor
imagine the grizzly paw on the vertebrae
special with a touch of smashed blueberries

3. drop in by off The Drive not out

passerby place the donation say it special
not that you are better or pretty broke
giveaway food is what others won't eat
people share what they don't want
cash flow assistance urgent not slow wait
can't pay the rent then sleep in the bushes
behind the veteran memorial where Indian died
it's Saturday Grandview Park feed in line up
food not bombs in the bowl of hippie soup
Diggers in the 60s memories fed the masses
ten right hands dig around spoiled veggies
remove bits of green mould on jalapeño bagel
in dishwater fingers touch soapy fingers
community cuisine is danger of infection
hepatitis target in a fork tine or cold water
is this the way raccoons scuffle for a meal
in Stanley Park then suffer rabies epidemic

4. yuppie begging bowl

passerby please notice us close up
beings stuck in camera lens we
pray poverty gets you to shell out
fill latte foam bowl with abundance

slow mo your fish flounder move
calculating cash flow mental scan
can hear spare change coins clink
musical chimes in purse or pocket
guess your plastic does not balance

because

      unwanted attention to debts
      you scoot by slow pan shot
      guilty with revulsion

we cause

      generous switch to far left
      hope hurried donation helps

camera roll plastic survivance level
at bank machine movie stake out
cut still broke expression ingenious

honest injun treaty bowl number one
block drumming manifesto but ears
ache from cotton swab frequent probe
practic tight ass titan squirm act
condo minimum convenience slamshot

move right along to bowl number two
white shiny too precious to let us bowl

      alley strikes air words
      warranty new diction
      help make a score again
      bowling for tidy dollars
      flush out settler set design

intrigue does anyone live on a budget
barely getting by pushed out on street
gross underestimate of mortality rate
women split disappear beg for life
interior exterior take on movie capital
we're good check for that missing gate
preview premiere prior to release date

tweak

Cuntajunta

Cunt do it alone cunt topped up cuntalina flow up spine
cunt drip drop that cunt let go smooth cunt silk hair leave it
to the cuntman is a man obsessed by cuntology cuntrary to
cunteraphobic afraid to say the word listen cuntajunta is only a
meeting of the minds of cunts denounce a couple of cunts ago
this damn cunt was saying I was a cunt like she wasn't or didn't
carry hers cuntly crotched must swear bigtime cunt off you pig
cunt right now cunta a cuntinent defined North American one
cunt two cunt three cunt times four cunts gives all these cunts
hanging around the cuntateria hoping for free cunt giveaway
to be cuntinued

egg clusive poem

ever fry a poem not like mine
particular basted low fat
computer zap cyber spaced embryo
sizzle words done
wok straight ahead
turn over tender
so white can't be runny
but yolk half done
flip out on fancy plate
huevos rancheros up

when boiling a poem
trust appropriate size utensil
done in hot weather conserve
sun energy best recreation
place one under write arm
sweat it until personal energy
efficiency kicks in enough vapour

coddling a poem warrants special
gourmet technique class conscious prep
keep low mumble jumble secret agent
instruction under breath strict privacy
counter intelligence breaking Canada
food rule somebody had to belabour
low propaganda possibility exegesis

Breed Apart

if bechance haggle over personal identity issue haunts
avoid taunts follow this homemade recipe to be hi bred

beat half breed self down to pulp & use necessary force
to mash identity until fluffy when if a slight peak forms
beat vigorously & use more Indian herbal ingredients
special dried wild stuff in cupboard for darker colour crust
add whiteman essence last for texture of this mad mix up
expose concoction to wind & let sit long enough for sun burn
eventual doneness test may well be stiff hard to the feel
so let's get real about who is real deal hard core indin

Indians & Half Breeds beat up each other accuse frequently
suspect breed in the family tree especially the one hanging
upside down on a branch calling for help getting down may
cause too much attention deserves a good smack but what if
that type goes red road devotee enters the sweat lodge special
care taken not to trip over pile up of non-native identity cluster
of euro yearnings for acceptance to avoid rejection must follow
proper preparation advised by leader "leave cultural baggage at
door" or "prescription note from therapist" along with offering
to qualify for enhancement & no fail guarantee nonrefundable

she ate lard & gophers diet for weeks to boost native awareness
heal the split within while reserve relatives had similar cuisine
except odd rabbit or vicarious born again experience on a
trapline Indian Act of 1951 partitions family one cousin part
Ukrainian has full status yet mother & aunt are enfranchised
with moniakwe label before Bill C-31 restores rights for exiles
to assume former existence as consenting Indian adults except
who wants to hear more "bs" which stands for "before status"
revelations similar dilemma to self-identification but provable
and demonstratable using this formula map genealogy

Beware Writer

Walking home I notice all the Beware Dog signs. Does this mean Beware Natives are Moving into the Neighbourhood? Or, is the message Watch Out This Is the Tough West End Part of the City? One house has three Beware Dog signs. Does that indicate three dogs? Beware Three Dog House.

I notice the fences. Some are chain link. Most of the houses have run down fences with Beware Dog signs. I see dogs in them. One is a puppy who doesn't bark. His huge chain has him caught by a kid's toy. He falls over on his back onto the plastic truck. He tries to right himself. Another dog sits at the window. Maybe longing to be outside. Another, a small collie, runs up to his fence and barks excitedly. He is across the street and the owner is in the yard.

Between the houses that have Beware Dog signs I see a Native place now and then. The most obvious have their kids playing outside on the porch or veranda. Some little ones are quite noisy and don't look at me when I pass by. Some are just quiet and stare. One little girl who is very fair has a very dirty little face. She wears only a small pair of shorts. She plays with her plastic trike getting herself more dirty. She has her own yard. One little girl across the street is hauling two of her friends in a wagon through a vacant cement lot.

Maybe the Beware Dogs arc inside their houses so that these children might play outside for a few hours each day. Maybe the German shepherds, Rottweilers, Pit Bulls and Dobermans are taking a day off. It is Sunday afternoon. It is their day not guard a home or property. Burglars may also be taking this Sunday afternoon to scout around the city. Are they casing up places to hit next week? At least, the dogs are not so evidently on duty.

Maybe everyone is afraid. I chose this street carefully. Looks pretty residential. Mostly houses with kids playing outside. These houses have families. Hey, families must live on the streets

I am avoiding. They live in big run down blocks managed by one big outfit like an insurance company. These managers of the ghetto don't give tenant insurance or life insurance to the people who provide the salaries for them. Real overlords. Sure the name of a gang. The people who run the worst part of the west end have private, protected families who are afraid to walk these streets.

(having chosen yet another name, nothing to brag about, she proposes being)

her other name did nothing except for cheque cashing, using just M was no option in the academy, internet gave her more names, specialized unlike M4 suggests collectivity while M Maybe revealed her abandonment issues how being afraid of M1, M2, M3, worse off was MF, M Maybe believes nothing, nothing is too good for her, what necessarily did not come before all number of last, middle, first names, she criticizes everything being unnamed she is nothing, she cannot curb enthusiasm for curling up in bed with names worthy of descent, she has not learned anything, except having a magic name is an amazing variation, 4 is not unlucky in the direction she moves. she catches on quickly to grab a name or any name, she may need to defend against her definitive person, her purpose being less exclusive, letting her true nature hang on every breath of her being aka short for always kindness around more naming

for marlon unas esguerra

cum cum how cum dat cums around even from behind

cum-fla-wid-me the skies choose symbiotic booze cruise wid me
transparent sway see thru gown shadow derrière sidewise flooze
cum-fla-wid-me the skies disguise our lives up size down prize
don drive dat car under influence go home alone let chauffeur
in slink white limo drive girl fla cruise fla low fla away ride way
lose exotic blues buzz pimp da hide pimp da pride height flight
just one commercial sets off fantasia an underclass entertainment
spree a black suited charlatan pours his alcohol beverage charm
invaded by his seductive chimerical stance transforms desire
croon da tune fla da moon mobility flair self fancy
fla da lady buzzard queen tiara envied by whirl
chancy girl shakes flamboyant headdress legacy
privileged plumes vary light stripe to dark rainbow
don't boast aloud or boast heart uppity comes round

manny booz ho cannot help notice wants her vanity to fly up his
ass his airline motto message to spread pleasure cum-fla-wid-me
crass for tricks sake he has to expose his prideful bum propel
brown cheeks stage a fatal attraction she cums slow circle wing
calculated to drop gently beside how beautiful dead he looks
delicious from behind rump saddle cause for celebration hold up
silver chalice to toast initiation of corpse composure such reeky
aroma from arsehole makes her look up close take quick peck
while her beak slides smoothly around the stink even still he does
not move but to semi relax sphincter extra calm porno pleasure
he's bit aroused she massages tiny little circles before her beak
inserts full tilt play and penetration so perverse shaman anus is
clued so cued sacred mischievous rite to suck absorb her entire
delicate head he must adjust her thrust inside surprise when bald
birdy wiggles free of snap shut buttock hold an all star wrestler
never that bold warn tease us to celebrate life responsible grasp
the turntable arm play record music humbly show off elegance

with minimal risk her crown is wrinkled anus like the one she
flew in to inspect without a cautious glance at expensive menu
stranger friction is how manny booz ho did not once let giggle
escape extent invasion caused her early onset of baldness for
culture vultures he entraps infamous fembot domination

Disabled diss away

downsized disease
as usual not under
down quilt cuddle
& bed bug bites

cool so damn cool
might get off cool down
all the time down
feather fluffy on inseam
more let down
down & out every day
down the tubes
down river without
proverbial paddle

keep one oar pull
in swirling rapids
or else flip out
drift down river
no return salmon
spawn origin
outdoors door slam
welcome except
greeting door mat
revolves intolerable
unnatural practice

broke down broken
press firm brake even
easy on day break
soon get the breaks
eventually give out
soon after alarm buzz
breakfast then let go

pacification flow in cup
java drowns depression
upper fix downward
lip corner curl composure
pictures no micro details
economic disparity jokefest
flat broke ndn tee shirt FBI
wear out me laugh me funny
onset episode spasms me

me nervous breakdown obvious
recite if nervous keep calm relax
you can do it you can do it words
discomfort leaves me disturbed
sly do not disturb oblivious me
suffering potential exposure
stressors whoever I induce
matrix of me being prophetic
just lay off stop networking
because you chum friend not so
trusting girl granny person trigger

feel unsafe in family influence
glare eyes do not see larger insidious
Indigenous down pressure endgame
odious economic differential self
wounded knee get over class based
mutilation no more amputations
mind muscle medication fussy
fixation down get down on it
stare eye red eye black eye whitey
de-stigmatize my wealth condition

internalized ableism racism classism
original mood swing not aboriginal
post-colonial syndrome failure
to remediate trajectory
F bomb exhortation

emergency endemic
betrayal ending
collective decision to deconstruct
realities dislocation loss of tropes

racism under dominant translation
internal gab no discernible accent
settler of colour alienation is often
de-skilled vulnerability lodged de-
attachment enclave ambivalence
tolerance toward expulsion okay
visit ethnic cleansed asylum but
double chocolate cake prizes
awards no surprise ndn resistance
surrounded with other dark skins
dark hand pushing tongue depressor
dark eyes grateful for occupation
resettlement yet somatic repression
lateral torture vicarious violins tune
apparatuses trafficked resilience non
virtual imprisonment friendly
cautious fear consents to therapy
modality fluent incongruous
those mandated report abuses
risk at-risk competence custom
sensitivity selective knowledge
ripples through flashbacks
accidental compassionates
me disease you cure all curator
make self-meaning cultural
make sense atonement grievous
casual truncated just a sec spew

increased caregiver connection
encompasses spiritual reconfigurations
be brief cogent counselling referral
intensified meaning fermented since
resemble reassemble remnant

historical trauma iteration ongoing
internecine conflict pauses to reflex
ignorant within wars scars coalition
group channelled metaphor mythology
makeover must be opinionated self
me witness diatribe diss ention

Indigenous Verse Ability

Right off, ingenious character needs to apply
any part-time genius rez identity on or off

Right on, dress accordingly use convenient
scalp wig or beaver hat trap appendage bag

Always, fuk wid Indin expert tease please
even if disabled walk with crutch is not even

Never, forget internal voice represents eternal
Injunaity croak sing songs of constant repetition

Remember, all ancestors big small fat lazy do-gooders
disguised helping professionals vary red alert alarm

Forget, ancestry breeds contempt for lesser bestials
why curse the drumstick butterballed to death apart

Come to it, pretend to copy another native vernacular
open the new age um biblical encyclopedia manual

Come off it, dust off the tonsil or operational vacancy
veer forward given our future is likely double doubt

Grab bundle, get a move on after all nomadism calls
visit worlds not on the internet or don't shop around

Let go, recognition reputation respite any reservations
linguistic liars documentaries what takes honest breath

Hang in there, even Riel knew how crazy monias were
stripped naked he showed them all he could not be hung

Laugh it up, not every day is a good day to genocide
not easy to chortle word choice snicker sounds digital

Laugh it off, easy enough to do if a feather is stuck
unusual place not tickly by any standard of remorse

Tweak

Warriors and Posse fight in prison
Native caregiver passenger on bus
must remove shank stuck in the back
sit ass down adjust granny gangbang
stoic stare in window of opportunity
shut up that is not a dagger before eyes
yes resemblance to machete butcher knife
say soul loss pain permits quickie forensic
mutual evisceration called lateral violence
Neechee Queens pass in Mad Cowz zone
got protection for bros and old lady escorts
flash a lighted camel smoke sends message
take care new comers move slow deliberate
drunk wrestling gives grandmas a workout
must patrol in case police show up stoned
occupied territory needs respectful address
without bed bug bites clean up crotch area
bear spray repellent in face works wonders
reduces gunshot wounds and details muggings
historical rapes for young girl vampire lust
discourse is not bloody forced intercourse
the mind grapple during classroom lecture
gather all ye spiritual buskers anal projection
realize face to face fear by avoidance ritual
now meaning if relatives do the killing fault
grab bags of federal funding why a concern
all euros are non generous trick or treaty teasers
New Jerusalem mimics Johannesburg slippage
apart hate have to cut it out pass that shank
for second generation Main Street creds image
tweak

Raving in the Hood

way back when in fact might be true another day

front of nose right there women muddle over story

how so gory women huddle borrow glam glory sorry

horror story what if told fabulous fable hype it princess

meets pimp prince lover type no fairy whore spell bind

resold retold twice say when old wives tales start once

upon time design how whore score rerun remake replay

old lady stories for sure not all grandma talk will bore us

does not won't don't gossip go sip up truth loose lip whine

so girlfriends must know the endings not even how solved

enough crime about women gone way down memory lane time

done prime chance to become even newsworthy story rehash

hey hang around listen to made up tale about she without she

never told her good points as she did not get too old to develop

on site insight remember no one told story about life friend

rough rave in the hood death just raven it after all up to no good

up to no good should we should no body guessed her body

does free pick up from crowd unique freak speak outcheek

find her around beer table hip hop she hung kinda out way out

not her fault mr one stripe fur covered guy find puts her on hold

twine over under blur of odorizer testosterone blast confuse

not her excuse me don't squeeze me again sir skunk embrace last

mistake she wasn't one to point out probable just blame perps

abc then v for vagina no actual intended victim game in tv view

was it only one time not so long ago did she play at risk knew

shame men grabbed between legs in sweat lodge dodge grope

now after burn incense is compassionate common sense

cocka doodle doo she saw you do exactly what you try do when

they do make us mind a quick screw to do sooner pay back

raven in the hood raven bitch best put out posse

pussy ki-ten rave in the hood really in bloody rage mood brood

what fur shit sake fur split sake f-u-r sake us forever ever figure

give out hint to girl half baked self time to wake up clever lady

f-u-r in sync forensic all four once f-u-r look out fur sense able

ndn time set on white cop watch schedule hours clock out wasted

overtime looking for sicko rude dude tattoo unglued crude prude fluid drink renewal time zest get rid buddy pest memory lane

go down kidnapped in parent zombie zap flasher meant her

flap & snap why take all crap rap flak run away no forward

address forget falling in sack start it all over again re-enact a kill

bungee been in bad hair day have we put one more still crumpet

in treaty toasted rights go get it over top flog it fine dandy as yet

fight nights succeed exceed next national day protest plan staged

complain refrain fries ketchup mustard came slow wait

with frequent wiener shoved in face his lone self in bugger buns

priest proofed any chance you want a chief similar odour

order up or do sweet tooth guys like aboriginal disorder better

don't bet on it they never transport her safe deposit place

easily convince her not to pick man on drive thru menu

available after he poses silent stand on her cold body in out field

listen up warrior outcry high volume pull the stake out vigil

ravage our hood would they do all over again in time to forget

Miigwech

*Onjida ningoding gimaanzhise, bagosedan idash
ji-maaninotooyan.*

There is a reason you have adversity, have hope you can alleviate
it.

— ROGER ROULETTE

Colin Smith for encouraging enthusiastic edit & van agit-poets
& academic allies & aboriginal writers group & Joy Asham,
storymaker supreme & rezblood cuz

Lawrence Paul's cover art & makes me guess "am I the red
blob?"

marie